South East Asia

From Thailand to the Philippines Enjoy Delicious South East Asian Cooking at Home

By
BookSumo Press
All rights reserved

Published by
http://www.booksumo.com

ENJOY THE RECIPES?

KEEP ON COOKING
WITH 6 MORE FREE COOKBOOKS!

Visit our website and simply enter your email address to join the club and receive your 6 cookbooks.

http://booksumo.com/magnet

https://www.instagram.com/booksumopress/

https://www.facebook.com/booksumo/

LEGAL NOTES

All Rights Reserved. No Part Of This Book May Be Reproduced Or Transmitted In Any Form Or By Any Means. Photocopying, Posting Online, And / Or Digital Copying Is Strictly Prohibited Unless Written Permission Is Granted By The Book's Publishing Company. Limited Use Of The Book's Text Is Permitted For Use In Reviews Written For The Public.

Table of Contents

Classical Pad Thai Noodles I 9

A Pesto From Thailand 10

Easy Hummus Thai Style 11

Classical Pad Thai Noodles II 12

Super Easy Coconut Soup Thai-Style 13

Curry Thai Inspired Chicken with Pineapple 14

Simple and Easy Classical Peanut Sauce 15

Vegetable Soup In Thailand 16

The Best Orange Thai Chicken 17

Thai Broccoli Mix 18

Uniquely Simple Cumber Soup with Thai Roots 19

BBQ Chicken Thai Style 20

Charong's Favorite Thai Soup of Ginger 21

Chicken Curry I 22

Chicken Curry II 23

A Thai Soup of Veggies 24

Chicken Burgers Re-Imagined From Thailand 25

Classical Shrimp In Thailand 26

Delightfully Thai Basil Chicken 27

A Pizza From Thailand 28

Spicy Thai Pasta 29

Fried Chicken from Thailand 30

Spicy Lime Shrimp 31

Honey Chili and Peanut Noodles 33

Maggie's Easy Coconut Soup 34

Peanut, Jalapeno, and Cucumber Salad 35

Khao Neeo Mamuang 36

Mango Curry Thai Chicken and Rice 37

Classical Peanut Sauce 38

Spicy Thai Cabbage and Shrimp 39

Pad Thai III 40

Thai Steak BBQ 41

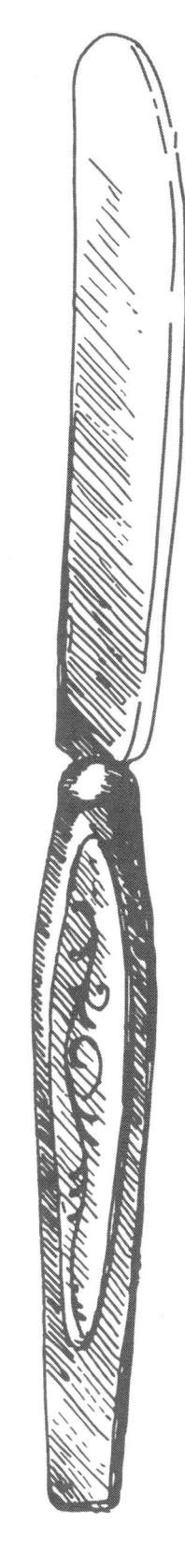

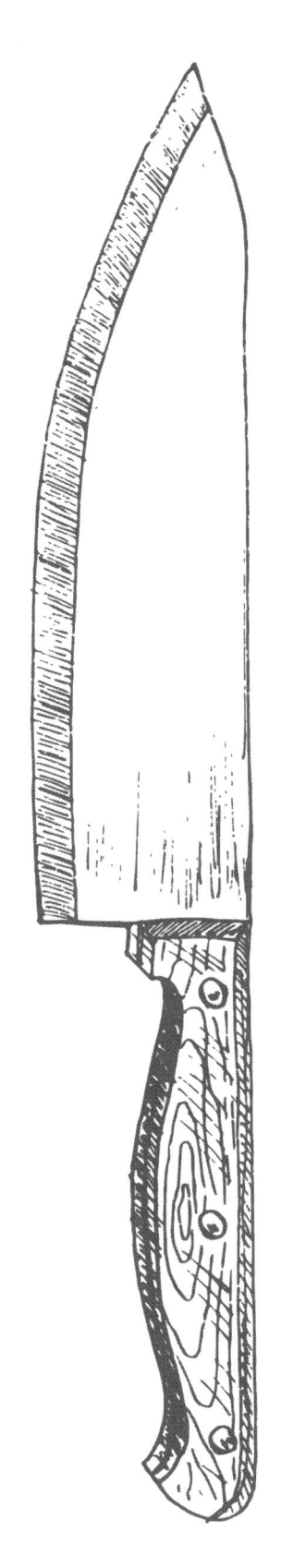

Thai Tofu Stir Fry 42

Sweet Coconut Rice 43

Southeast Asian Chicken Curry 44

Tilapia from Thailand 45

Maggie's Easy Thai Style Fried Rice 46

Thai Ginger Fish Patties 47

Fish Cakes from Thailand 48

Nam Prik Ong 49

Honey and Chili Chicken Legs 50

Bangkok Ginger Beef 51

Thai Pizza 52

Filipino Oxtail Stew 53

Buko I 54

Biko 55

Tulya 56

Chicken Adobo 57

Barbecued Spareribs 58

Empanada Turkey Filling 59

Filipino Melon Dessert I 60

Salmon Stew 61

Fried Tulingan 62

Filipino Fruit Salad 63

Avocado Milkshakes in the Philippines 64

Singkamas 65

Picadillo Filipino 66

Fish Sinigang 67

Sinigang Na Baka 68

Melon Chiller 69

Filipino Chicken Stew 70

Champorado 71

Maja Blanca Maiz 72

Cassava Cake 73

Butter Cookies in Philippines 74

Filipino Melon Dessert II 75

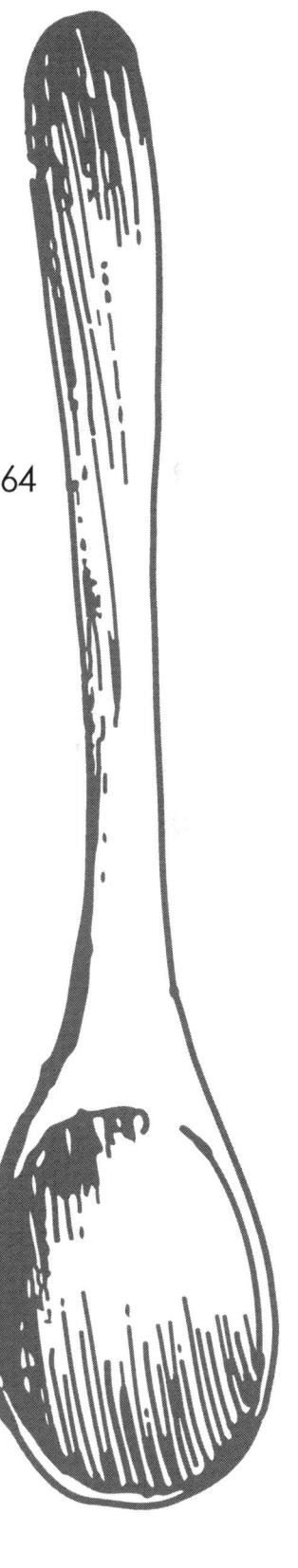

Chocolate-Orange Rice Pudding 76

Corned Beef Hash In the Philippines 77

Corned Beef Waffles 78

Mango Bread 79

Guinataan Hito 80

Buko II 81

Classical Pad Thai Noodles I

Prep Time: 30 mins
Total Time: 2 hrs

Servings per Recipe: 4
Calories	397 kcal
Carbohydrates	39.5 g
Cholesterol	41 mg
Fat	23.3 g
Protein	13.2 g
Sodium	1234 mg

Ingredients

- 2/3 C. dried rice vermicelli
- 1/4 C. peanut oil
- 2/3 C. thinly sliced firm tofu
- 1 large egg, beaten
- 4 cloves garlic, finely chopped
- 1/4 C. vegetable broth
- 2 tbsps fresh lime juice
- 2 tbsps soy sauce
- 1 tbsp white sugar
- 1 tsp salt
- 1/2 tsp dried red chili flakes
- 3 tbsps chopped peanuts
- 1 pound bean sprouts, divided
- 3 green onions, whites cut thinly across and greens sliced into thin lengths - divided
- 3 tbsps chopped peanuts
- 2 limes, cut into wedges for garnish

Directions

1. Put rice vermicelli noodles in hot water for about 30 minutes before draining the water.
2. Cook tofu in hot oil until golden brown before draining it with paper tower.
3. Reserve 1 tbsp of oil for later use and cook egg in the remaining hot oil until done, and set them aside for later use.
4. Now cook noodles and garlic in the hot reserved oil, while coating them well with this oil along the way.
5. In this pan containing noodles; add tofu, salt, chili flakes, egg and 3 tbsps peanuts, and mix all this very thoroughly.
6. Also add bean sprouts and green onion into it, while reserving some for the garnishing purposes.
7. Cook all this for two minutes before transferring to a serving platter.
8. Garnish this with peanuts and the reserved vegetables before placing some lime wedges around the platter to make this dish more attractive.
9. Serve.

A PESTO
From Thailand

Prep Time: 10 mins
Total Time: 10 mins

Servings per Recipe: 12
Calories	84 kcal
Carbohydrates	3.4 g
Cholesterol	0 mg
Fat	7.4 g
Protein	1.9 g
Sodium	197 mg

Ingredients

- 1 bunch cilantro
- 1/4 C. peanut butter
- 3 cloves garlic, minced
- 3 tbsps extra-virgin olive oil
- 2 tbsps minced fresh ginger
- 1 1/2 tbsps fish sauce
- 1 tbsp brown sugar
- 1/2 tsp cayenne pepper

Directions

1. Put all the ingredients that are mentioned above in a blender and blend it until you see that the required smoothness is achieved.

Easy Hummus Thai Style

Prep Time: 15 mins
Total Time: 30 mins

Servings per Recipe: 12
Calories   142 kcal
Carbohydrates   13.8 g
Cholesterol   0 mg
Fat   9.4 g
Protein   3.9 g
Sodium   315 mg

Ingredients

1/4 C. coconut oil
2 large cloves garlic, very thinly sliced
2 C. cooked garbanzo beans
1/4 C. fresh lime juice
1/4 C. peanut butter
1/4 C. coconut milk
1/4 C. sweet chili sauce
1/4 C. minced lemon grass
1/4 C. minced fresh Thai basil leaves
1 tbsp grated fresh ginger
2 tsps green curry paste
1 jalapeno pepper, minced
1/2 tsp salt
1 pinch cayenne pepper (optional)
1 pinch chili powder (optional)

Directions

1. Cook garlic in hot coconut oil for about one minute and transfer it to a bowl.
2. Put cooled garlic mixture, lime juice, coconut milk, chili sauce, lemon grass, basil, ginger, curry paste, garbanzo beans, jalapeno pepper, salt, peanut butter, cayenne pepper and chili in a blender and blend it until you find that it is smooth.
3. Serve.

CLASSICAL
Pad Thai Noodles II

Prep Time: 15 mins
Total Time: 25 mins

Servings per Recipe: 4
Calories   352 kcal
Carbohydrates   46.8 g
Cholesterol   46 mg
Fat   15 g
Protein   9.2 g
Sodium   335 mg

Ingredients

1 (6.75 ounce) package thin rice noodles
2 tbsps vegetable oil
3 ounces fried tofu, sliced into thin strips
1 clove garlic, minced
1 egg
1 tbsp soy sauce
1 pinch white sugar
2 tbsps chopped peanuts
1 C. fresh bean sprouts
1 tbsp chopped fresh cilantro
1 lime, cut into wedges

Directions

1. In a heatproof bowl containing noodles, pour boiling water and let it stand as it is for about five minutes before draining the water and setting it aside for later use.
2. Fry garlic in hot oil until brown before adding noodles frying it for about one minute.
3. Now add egg into it and break it up when it starts to get solid, and mix it well into the noodles.
4. Now add soy sauce, tofu, cilantro, bean sprouts, sugar and peanuts into it and mix it well.
5. Remove from heat and add lime wedges just before you serve.

Super Easy Coconut Soup Thai-Style

Prep Time: 15 mins
Total Time: 40 mins

Servings per Recipe: 8	
Calories	314 kcal
Carbohydrates	17.2 g
Cholesterol	86 mg
Fat	21.6 g
Protein	15.3 g
Sodium	523 mg

Ingredients

1 pound medium shrimp - peeled and deveined
2 (13.5 ounce) cans canned coconut milk
2 C. water
1 (1 inch) piece galangal, thinly sliced
4 stalks lemon grass, bruised and chopped
10 kaffir lime leaves, torn in half
1 pound shiitake mushrooms, sliced
1/4 C. lime juice
3 tbsps fish sauce
1/4 C. brown sugar
1 tsp curry powder
1 tbsp green onion, thinly sliced
1 tsp dried red pepper flakes

Directions

1. Cook shrimp in boiling water until tender.
2. Put coconut milk, water, lime leaves, galangal and lemon grass in a large sized pan and heat it up for about 10 minutes before transferring the coconut milk into a new pan, while discarding all the spices.
3. Heat up shiitake mushrooms in the coconut milk for five minutes before adding lime juice, curry powder, brown sugar and fish sauce into it.
4. When you want to serve it, heat up the shrimp in this soup for some time before pouring this into serving bowls.

CURRY
Thai Inspired Chicken with Pineapple

Prep Time: 15 mins
Total Time: 50 mins

Servings per Recipe: 6
Calories 623 kcal
Carbohydrates 77.5 g
Cholesterol 20 mg
Fat 34.5 g
Protein 20.3 g
Sodium 781 mg

Ingredients

2 C. uncooked jasmine rice
1 quart water
1/4 C. red curry paste
2 (13.5 ounce) cans coconut milk
2 skinless, boneless chicken breast halves - cut into thin strips
3 tbsps fish sauce
1/4 C. white sugar
1 1/2 C. sliced bamboo shoots, drained
1/2 red bell pepper, julienned
1/2 green bell pepper, julienned
1/2 small onion, chopped
1 C. pineapple chunks, drained

Directions

1. Bring the mixture of rice and water to boil before turning the heat down to low and cooking for 25 minutes.
2. Add coconut milk, bamboo shoots, chicken, sugar and fish sauce to the mixture of curry paste and 1 can coconut milk in a pan before bringing all this to boil and cooking for 15 minutes.
3. Into this mixture, add red bell pepper, onion and green bell pepper, and cook all this for ten more minutes or until you see that the peppers are tender.
4. Add pineapple after removing from heat and serve this on top of cooked rice.

Simple and Easy Classical Peanut Sauce

Prep Time: 10 mins
Total Time: 10 mins

Servings per Recipe: 6	
Calories	130 kcal
Carbohydrates	9.8 g
Cholesterol	3 mg
Fat	9.5 g
Protein	2.7 g
Sodium	529 mg

Ingredients

- 1/4 C. creamy peanut butter
- 3 cloves garlic, minced
- 1/4 C. brown sugar
- 1/4 C. mayonnaise
- 1/4 C. soy sauce
- 2 tbsps fresh lemon juice

Directions

1. Whisk all the ingredients that are mentioned above in a medium sized bowl and refrigerate it for at least two hours before you serve it to anyone.

VEGETABLE SOUP
In Thailand

Prep Time: 15 mins
Total Time: 1 hr 30 mins

Servings per Recipe: 12
Calories   183 kcal
Carbohydrates   21.4 g
Cholesterol   < 1 mg
Fat   7.4 g
Protein   4.4 g
Sodium   749 mg

Ingredients

1 C. uncooked brown rice
2 C. water
3 tbsps olive oil
1 sweet onion, chopped
4 cloves garlic, minced
1/4 C. chopped fresh ginger root
1 C. chopped carrots
4 C. chopped broccoli
1 red bell pepper, diced
1 (14 ounce) can light coconut milk
6 C. vegetable broth

1 C. white wine
3 tbsps fish sauce
2 tbsps soy sauce
3 Thai chili peppers
2 tbsps chopped fresh lemon grass
1 tbsp Thai pepper garlic sauce
1 tsp saffron
3/4 C. plain yogurt
fresh cilantro, for garnish

Directions

1. Bring the mixture of rice and water to boil before turning the heat down to low and cooking for 45 minutes.
2. Cook ginger, carrots, garlic and onion in hot olive oil for about five minutes before you add broccoli, coconut milk, broth, wine, soy sauce, Thai chili peppers, red bell pepper, lemon grass, fish sauce, garlic sauce, and saffron into it and cook for another 25 minutes.
3. Now blend this soup in batches in a blender until you get the required smoothness.
4. Mix yoghurt and cooked rice very thoroughly with this soup.
5. Garnish with cilantro before you serve.

The Best Orange Thai Chicken

Prep Time: 15 mins
Total Time: 40 mins

Servings per Recipe: 12
Calories   427 kcal
Carbohydrates   37.1 g
Cholesterol   32 mg
Fat   24.3 g
Protein   18.4 g
Sodium   1360 mg

Ingredients

2 tbsps olive oil
3 carrots, cut into matchsticks
1/2 tsp minced fresh ginger root
1 clove garlic, minced
2 tbsps olive oil
2 skinless, boneless chicken breast halves, cut into small pieces
1/2 C. water
1/2 C. peanuts
1/3 C. orange juice
1/3 C. soy sauce
1/3 C. brown sugar
2 tbsps ketchup
1 tsp crushed red pepper flakes
2 tbsps cornstarch

Directions

1. Cook carrots, garlic and ginger in hot olive oil for about 5 minutes before transferring it to a bowl.
2. Cook chicken in hot olive oil for about 10 minutes before adding carrot mixture, water, brown sugar, orange juice, soy sauce, peanuts, ketchup, and red pepper flakes into this, and cooking for another 5 minutes.
3. Take out ¼ C. of sauce from the pan and add cornstarch into it.
4. Add this cornstarch mixture back to the chicken and cook until you see that the required thickness has been reached.

THAI
Broccoli Mix

🥘 Prep Time: 10 mins
🕒 Total Time: 30 mins

Servings per Recipe: 4
Calories	315 kcal
Carbohydrates	8.2 g
Cholesterol	65 mg
Fat	18.9 g
Protein	28.3 g
Sodium	275 mg

Ingredients

- 2 tbsps olive oil
- 2 large skinless, boneless chicken breast halves, cut into bite-size pieces
- 1 (12 ounce) package broccoli coleslaw mix
- 1 tsp sesame oil, or to taste
- 1/2 C. water
- 1/2 C. peanut sauce (such as House of Tsang®), or to taste
- 1 pinch salt to taste

Directions

1. Cook chicken in hot olive oil for about 5 minutes before you add water, broccoli and sesame oil.
2. Cook this on medium heat for about 15 minutes or until you see that the broccoli slaw is tender.
3. Do add some peanut sauce and salt according to your taste before serving.

A Uniquely Simple Cumber Soup with Thai Roots

Prep Time: 15 mins
Total Time: 45 mins

Servings per Recipe: 4
Calories   67 kcal
Carbohydrates   6.8 g
Cholesterol   3 mg
Fat   4 g
Protein   1.7 g
Sodium   702 mg

Ingredients

1 tbsp vegetable oil
3 cucumbers, peeled and diced
1/2 C. chopped green onion
2 1/2 C. chicken broth
1 1/2 tbsps lemon juice
1 tsp white sugar
salt and ground black pepper to taste

Directions

1. Cook cucumber in hot olive oil for about 5 minutes before adding green onions and cooking for another five minutes.
2. Add chicken broth, sugar and lemon juice into it before bringing all this to boil.
3. Turn down the heat to low and cook for another 20 minutes before adding salt and black pepper according to your taste.
4. Serve.

BBQ CHICKEN
Thai Style

🥣 Prep Time: 15 mins
🕐 Total Time: 4 hrs 45 mins

Servings per Recipe: 4
Calories   564 kcal
Carbohydrates   52.4 g
Cholesterol   230 mg
Fat   19.3 g
Protein   46.3 g
Sodium   375 mg

Ingredients

1 bunch fresh cilantro with roots
3 cloves garlic, peeled
3 small red hot chili peppers, seeded and chopped
1 tsp ground turmeric
1 tsp curry powder
1 tbsp white sugar
1 pinch salt
3 tbsps fish sauce
1 (3 pound) chicken, cut into pieces
1/4 C. coconut milk

Directions

1. At first you need to set a grill or grilling plate to medium heat and put some oil before starting anything else.
2. Put minced cilantro roots, salt, leaves, chili peppers, curry powder, turmeric, sugar, fish sauce, garlic in a blender and blend until you see that the required smoothness is achieved.
3. Combine this paste and chicken in large bowl, and refrigerate it for at least three hours for margination.
4. Cook this on the preheated grill for about 15 minutes each side or until tender, while brushing it regularly with coconut milk.
5. Serve.
6. NOTE: Adjust grilling times accordingly if using a grilling plate instead of a conventional grill.

Charong's Favorite Thai Soup of Ginger

Prep Time: 15 mins
Total Time: 25 mins

Servings per Recipe: 4	
Calories	415 kcal
Carbohydrates	7.3 g
Cholesterol	29 mg
Fat	39 g
Protein	14.4 g
Sodium	598 mg

Ingredients

- 3 C. coconut milk
- 2 C. water
- 1/2 pound skinless, boneless chicken breast halves - cut into thin strips
- 3 tbsps minced fresh ginger root
- 2 tbsps fish sauce, or to taste
- 1/4 C. fresh lime juice
- 2 tbsps sliced green onions
- 1 tbsp chopped fresh cilantro

Directions

1. Bring the mixture of coconut milk and water to boil before adding chicken strips, and cooking it for three minutes on medium heat or until you see that the chicken is cooked through.
2. Now add ginger, green onions, lime juice, cilantro and fish sauce into it.
3. Mix it well and serve.

CHICKEN
Curry I

🥣 Prep Time: 15 mins
🕐 Total Time: 55 mins

Servings per Recipe: 6
Calories 500 kcal
Carbohydrates 22.1 g
Cholesterol 58 mg
Fat 36.1 g
Protein 25.8 g
Sodium 437 mg

Ingredients

1 tbsp olive oil
3 tbsps Thai yellow curry paste (such as Mae Ploy®)
1 pound cooked skinless, boneless chicken breast, cut into bite-size pieces
2 (14 ounce) cans coconut milk
1 C. chicken stock
1 yellow onion, chopped
3 small red potatoes, cut into cubes, or as needed
3 red Thai chili peppers, chopped with seeds, or more to taste
1 tsp fish sauce

Directions

1. Mix curry paste in hot oil before adding chicken and coating it well.
2. Add 1 can coconut milk and cook it for five minutes before adding the rest of the coconut milk, onion, potatoes, chicken stock and chili peppers into it and bringing all this to boil.
3. Turn the heat down to low and cook for 25 minutes or until the potatoes are tender.
4. Add fish sauce into before serving.
5. Enjoy.

Chicken Curry II

Prep Time: 15 mins
Total Time: 35 mins

Servings per Recipe: 4
Calories   621 kcal
Carbohydrates   86.7 g
Cholesterol   91 mg
Fat   19.4 g
Protein   35.2 g
Sodium   316 mg

Ingredients

1 tbsp canola oil
2 tbsps green curry paste
1 pound boneless skinless chicken breasts, cut into bite-size pieces
1 small onion, thinly sliced
1 red pepper, cut into thin strips, then cut crosswise in half
1 green pepper, cut into thin strips, then cut crosswise in half
4 ounces cream cheese, cubed
1/4 C. milk
1/8 tsp white pepper
2 C. hot cooked long-grain white rice

Directions

1. Combine curry paste and hot oil before adding chicken and onions.
2. Cook this for about 8 minutes before adding green and red peppers, and cooking for another five minutes.
3. Now add cream cheese, white pepper and milk, and cook until you see that the cheese has melted.
4. Serve this on top of rice.
5. Enjoy.

A THAI
Soup of Veggies

Prep Time: 15 mins
Total Time: 50 mins

Servings per Recipe: 5
Calories	310 kcal
Carbohydrates	22.9 g
Cholesterol	55 mg
Fat	22.4 g
Protein	8.5 g
Sodium	147 mg

Ingredients

- 1/4 C. butter
- 6 tomatoes, peeled and quartered
- 3 zucchini, cut into chunks
- 1 yellow onion, cut in half and quartered
- 1 red bell pepper, chopped
- 3 cloves garlic, roughly chopped
- 1/4 C. chopped fresh cilantro leaves
- 1 tbsp chopped fresh basil (preferably Thai basil)
- 1 tbsp lime juice
- 1 pinch salt
- 2 1/2 C. milk
- 3 tbsps coconut butter
- 1 tbsp curry powder
- 1/4 tsp ground turmeric
- 1/4 tsp ground ginger
- 1/8 tsp ground cumin
- 1 bay leaf
- 5 tbsps heavy whipping cream (optional)

Directions

1. Cook tomatoes, zucchini, onion, garlic, cilantro, red bell pepper, basil, lime juice, and salt in hot butter for about 25 minutes before transferring it to a blender and blending it until the required smoothness is achieved.
2. Cook milk, curry powder, turmeric, ginger, coconut butter, cumin, and bay leaf in the same pan for about 5 minutes or until you see that coconut butter has melted.
3. At the very end, add blended vegetables into it and cook for five more minutes.
4. Garnish with heavy cream before serving.

Chicken Burgers Re-Imagined From Thailand

Prep Time: 15 mins
Total Time: 30 mins

Servings per Recipe: 8
Calories	612 kcal
Carbohydrates	50.9 g
Cholesterol	80 mg
Fat	35.4 g
Protein	36.5 g
Sodium	859 mg

Ingredients

- 1 C. mayonnaise
- 1/4 C. flaked coconut, finely chopped
- 1 tbsp chopped fresh mint
- 2 pounds ground chicken
- 2 1/2 C. panko bread crumbs
- 1/2 C. Thai peanut sauce
- 2 tbsps red curry paste
- 2 tbsps minced green onion
- 2 tbsps minced fresh parsley
- 2 tsps soy sauce
- 3 cloves garlic, minced
- 2 tsps lemon juice
- 2 tsps lime juice
- 1 tbsp hot pepper sauce
- 8 hamburger buns, split and toasted

Directions

1. At first you need to set a grill or grilling plate to medium heat and put some oil before starting anything else. Refrigerate a mixture of mayonnaise, mint and coconut for one hour. Combine ground chicken, Thai peanut sauce, curry paste, parsley, soy sauce, garlic, lemon juice, green onion, panko crumbs, lime juice, and hot pepper sauce in large sized bowl. Cook this on the preheated grill for about 8 minutes each side or until tender.
2. Serve this with toasted bun.
3. NOTE: Adjust grilling times accordingly if using a grilling plate instead of a conventional grill.

CLASSICAL
Shrimp In Thailand

Prep Time: 10 mins
Total Time: 30 mins

Servings per Recipe: 4
Calories	289 kcal
Carbohydrates	8.2 g
Cholesterol	173 mg
Fat	20.1 g
Protein	20.9 g
Sodium	502 mg

Ingredients

4 cloves garlic, peeled
1 (1 inch) piece fresh ginger root
1 fresh jalapeno pepper, seeded
1/2 tsp salt
1/2 tsp ground turmeric
2 tbsps vegetable oil
1 medium onion, diced
1 pound medium shrimp - peeled and deveined
2 tomatoes, seeded and diced
1 C. coconut milk
3 tbsps chopped fresh basil leaves

Directions

1. Blend the mixture of garlic, turmeric, ginger and jalapeno in a blender until the required smoothness is achieved.
2. Cook onion in hot oil for a few minutes before adding spice paste and cooking for another few minutes.
3. Cook shrimp for a few minutes in it before adding tomatoes and coconut milk, and cooking it for five minutes covered with lid.
4. Now cook for five more minutes without lid to get the sauce thick.
5. Also add some fresh basil at the last minute.
6. Serve.

Delightfully Thai Basil Chicken

Prep Time: 15 mins
Total Time: 20 mins

Servings per Recipe: 4
Calories	273 kcal
Carbohydrates	16.5 g
Cholesterol	69 mg
Fat	10.7 g
Protein	29.4 g
Sodium	769 mg

Ingredients

- 2 tbsps peanut oil
- 1/4 C. minced garlic
- 1 pound ground chicken breast
- 12 Thai chilis, sliced into thin rings
- 2 tsps black soy sauce
- 2 tbsps fish sauce
- 1 C. fresh basil leaves

Directions

1. Cook garlic in hot peanut oil for about twenty seconds before adding ground chicken and cooking for another two minutes or until the chicken loses any pinkness.
2. Now add sliced chilies, fish sauce and soy sauce into it before cooking for 15 seconds to get the chilies tender.
3. At the very end, add basil and cook until you see that basil has wilted.
4. Serve.

A PIZZA
From Thailand

Prep Time: 10 mins
Total Time: 20 mins

Servings per Recipe: 8
Calories	396 kcal
Carbohydrates	33.3 g
Cholesterol	37 mg
Fat	20.2 g
Protein	24.2 g
Sodium	545 mg

Ingredients

1 (12 inch) pre-baked pizza crust
1 (7 ounce) jar peanut sauce
1/4 C. peanut butter
8 ounces cooked skinless, boneless chicken breast halves, cut into strips
1 C. shredded Italian cheese blend
1 bunch green onions, chopped

1/2 C. fresh bean sprouts(optional)
1/2 C. shredded carrot(optional)
1 tbsp chopped roasted peanuts (optional)

Directions

1. Preheat your oven to 400 degrees F.
2. Spread a mixture of peanut sauce and peanut butter over the pizza crust and also put some strips of chicken, green onions and cheese.
3. Bake in the preheated oven for about 12 minutes or until the cheese has melted.
4. Garnish with carrot shreds, peanuts and sprouts.
5. Serve.

Spicy Thai Pasta

Prep Time: 15 mins
Total Time: 20 mins

Servings per Recipe: 8
Calories   564 kcal
Carbohydrates   52.4 g
Cholesterol   230 mg
Fat   19.3 g
Protein   46.3 g
Sodium   375 mg

Ingredients

1 (12 ounce) package rice vermicelli
1 large tomato, diced
2 pounds cooked shrimp, peeled and deveined

4 green onions, diced 1 1/2 C. prepared Thai peanut sauce

Directions

1. Add rice vermicelli into boiling water and cook for about five minutes or until done.
2. Combine this rice with tomato, peanut sauce, green onions and shrimp very thoroughly in a medium sized bowl before refrigerating for at least eight hours.

FRIED CHICKEN
from Thailand

🥣 Prep Time: 15 mins
🕐 Total Time: 4 hrs 50 mins

Servings per Recipe: 4
Calories	1032 kcal
Fat	47.5 g
Carbohydrates	102.1g
Protein	76.1 g
Cholesterol	1292 mg
Sodium	1428 mg

Ingredients

1/2 C. honey mustard
1/2 C. sweet chili sauce
2 eggs, beaten
sea salt to taste
12 chicken drumsticks
4 C. panko bread crumbs
4 C. vegetable oil for frying

Directions

1. Get a bowl, combine: sea salt, honey mustard, eggs, and chili sauce.
2. Stir the mix until it is smooth and even then pour the mix into a plastic bag.
3. Add your chicken to the bag and squeeze out all the air. Seal the bag then place everything in the fridge for 5 hrs.
4. Now set your oven to 350 degrees before doing anything else.
5. Get a dish layer your bread crumbs in it. Coat your pieces of chicken with the flour then begin to fry the chicken in hot veggie oil for 9 mins.
6. Now place the meat on a cookie sheet and cook everything in the oven for 40 mins.
7. Enjoy.

Spicy Lime Shrimp

⏲ Prep Time: 1 hr
🕐 Total Time: 1 hr 24 mins

Servings per Recipe: 8
Calories   535 kcal
Fat   39.4 g
Carbohydrates   14.9 g
Protein   29.2 g
Cholesterol   173 mg
Sodium   648 mg

Ingredients

- 1/4 C. minced lemon grass (white part only)
- 1/4 C. minced fresh ginger root
- 2 tbsps minced garlic
- 1/4 tbsp chopped fresh cilantro
- 1 Thai or serrano chili pepper, minced
- 3/4 C. peanut or canola oil
- 2 lbs extra large shrimp (16 - 20), peeled and deveined, tail left on
- 1/4 C. lime juice
- 1/4 C. rice wine vinegar
- 1/2 C. mirin (Japanese sweet wine)
- 2 tbsps dark soy sauce
- 2 tbsps cold water
- 3 tbsps grated lime zest
- 1 tbsp minced fresh ginger root
- 2 tsps fish sauce
- 2 fresh Thai or Serrano chili, seeds removed
- 2 tsps minced garlic
- 1/2 C. smooth, unsalted peanut butter
- 1/4 C. peanut oil
- 2 tbsps chopped fresh mint
- 1 tbsp chopped fresh cilantro
- 1/4 C. unsalted roasted peanuts, chopped
- Kosher salt to taste

Directions

1. Get a bowl, combine: 3/4 C. of peanut oil, lemon grass, 1 minced chili, 1/4 C. of ginger, cilantro, and garlic.
2. Stir in the shrimp to the mix and place a covering of plastic over everything.
3. Let the bowl sit for 40 mins.
4. At the same time begin to pulse the following in a food processor: water, lime juice, soy sauce, mirin, and rice vinegar.
5. Get the mix smooth then add in: peanut butter, lime zest, garlic, 1 tbsp ginger, 2 chili peppers, and fish sauce.
6. Continue pulsing until everything is smooth again.
7. Now set the processor to a low speed and gradually add in the peanut oil in an even stream.

8. Once the mix is creamy enter everything into a bowl. Then add in: pepper, mint, salt, cilantro, and chopped peanuts.
9. Cook your pieces of fish on the grill for 4 mins each side. When eating the shrimp dip the pieces in the peanut sauce.
10. Enjoy.

Honey Chili and Peanut Noodles

Prep Time: 15 mins
Total Time: 25 mins

Servings per Recipe: 4
Calories	330 kcal
Fat	12 g
Carbohydrates	46.8g
Protein	10.7 g
Cholesterol	0 mg
Sodium	1188 mg

Ingredients

- 1/2 C. chicken broth
- 1 1/2 tbsps minced fresh ginger root
- 3 tbsps soy sauce
- 3 tbsps peanut butter
- 1 1/2 tbsps honey
- 2 tsps hot chili paste (optional)
- 3 cloves garlic, minced
- 8 oz. Udon noodles
- 1/4 C. chopped green onions
- 1/4 C. chopped peanuts

Directions

1. Boil your noodles in water for 9 mins then remove all the liquids.
2. At the same time begin to stir and heat the following in a pan: garlic, broth, chili paste, ginger, honey, soy sauce, and peanut butter.
3. Once the mix is hot and smooth add in your noodles when they are finished. Then stir everything to evenly distribute the sauce.
4. Now top the noodles with some peanuts and onions.
5. Enjoy.

MAGGIE'S Easy Coconut Soup

Prep Time: 35 mins
Total Time: 1 hr 5 mins

Servings per Recipe: 8
Calories   375 kcal
Fat   33.2 g
Carbohydrates   9.4g
Protein   13.7 g
Cholesterol   89 mg
Sodium   1059 mg

Ingredients

- 1 tbsp vegetable oil
- 2 tbsps grated fresh ginger
- 1 stalk lemon grass, minced
- 2 tsps red curry paste
- 4 C. chicken broth
- 3 tbsps fish sauce
- 1 tbsp light brown sugar
- 3 (13.5 oz.) cans coconut milk
- 1/2 lb fresh shiitake mushrooms, sliced
- 1 lb medium shrimp - peeled and deveined
- 2 tbsps fresh lime juice
- salt to taste
- 1/4 C. chopped fresh cilantro

Directions

1. Stir fry your curry paste, lemongrass, and ginger in oil for 2 mins then add in the broth while continuing to stir everything.
2. Add in the brown sugar and fish sauce and let the contents gently boil for 17 mins.
3. Now add the mushrooms and the coconut milk.
4. Continue cooking everything for 7 more min.
5. Then combine in the shrimp and let the fish cook for 7 mins until it is fully done.
6. Now add some cilantro, salt, and lime juice.
7. Enjoy.

Peanut, Jalapeno, and Cucumber Salad

Prep Time: 15 mins
Total Time: 45 mins

Servings per Recipe: 4
Calories	238 kcal
Fat	9.4 g
Carbohydrates	37.1g
Protein	5.8 g
Cholesterol	0 mg
Sodium	1751 mg

Ingredients

- 3 large cucumbers, peeled, halved lengthwise, seeded, and cut into 1/4-inch slices
- 1 tbsp salt
- 1/2 C. white sugar
- 1/2 C. rice wine vinegar
- 2 jalapeno peppers, seeded and chopped
- 1/4 C. chopped cilantro
- 1/2 C. chopped peanuts

Directions

1. Get a perforated bowl and in the sink combine your salt and cucumbers.
2. Let the mix sit for 40 mins then run the veggies under some fresh water.
3. Now dry everything with some paper towels.
4. Get a bowl, combine: vinegar and sugar.
5. Continue mixing everything until the sugar is fully incorporated with the vinegar then combine in: cilantro, jalapenos, and cucumbers.
6. Top everything with some peanuts.
7. Enjoy.

KHAO NEEO Mamuang (Thai Sweet Rice)

Prep Time: 10 mins
Total Time: 1 hr 30 mins

Servings per Recipe: 4
Calories   817 kcal
Fat   26 g
Carbohydrates   144.3g
Protein   8.4 g
Cholesterol   0 mg
Sodium   458 mg

Ingredients

1 1/2 C. uncooked short-grain white rice
2 C. water
1 1/2 C. coconut milk
1 C. white sugar
1/2 tsp salt
1/2 C. coconut milk
1 tbsp white sugar
1/4 tsp salt

1 tbsp tapioca starch
3 mangos, peeled and sliced
1 tbsp toasted sesame seeds

Directions

1. Get your rice boiling in water, set the heat to low, place a lid on the pot, and let the rice cook for 17 mins.
2. At the same time get the following boiling: 1/2 tsp salt, 1.5 C. coconut milk, and 1 C. of sugar.
3. Stir the mix as it heats. Then once everything is boiling shut the heat.
4. Add the rice to the mix once it is done cooking, stir the mix, and let everything sit for 60 mins.
5. Get a separate pan and begin to get the following boiling: 1/4 tsp salt, 1/2 C. coconut milk, 1 tbsp sugar, and tapioca.
6. Once the mix has boiled for a few mins and is thick layer your rice on a plate.
7. Place some mango on top of the rice and top everything with the sauce.
8. Garnish the dish with the sesame seeds.
9. Enjoy.

Mango Curry Thai Chicken and Rice

Prep Time: 10 mins
Total Time: 55 mins

Servings per Recipe: 6
Calories   669 kcal
Fat   26.3 g
Carbohydrates   90.5g
Protein   22.6 g
Cholesterol   32 mg
Sodium   1785 mg

Ingredients

- 3 C. water
- 1 1/2 C. jasmine rice
- 1 tsp salt
- 3 skinless, boneless chicken breast halves
- 1/2 C. soy sauce
- 1 tbsp water, or as desired
- 1 (14 oz.) can coconut milk
- 1 C. white sugar
- 2 tbsps curry powder
- 1 mango - peeled, seeded, and diced
- 2 C. clover sprouts, or to taste
- 1 C. finely chopped cashews
- 1 bunch fresh cilantro, finely chopped
- 4 green onions, chopped

Directions

1. Get your rice boiling in water with some salt. Once the mix is boiling set the heat to low, place a lid on the pot, and let the rice cook for 17 mins.
2. Now shut the heat and let everything stand for 7 mins.
3. Over heat, in a separate pot, combine your soy sauce, chicken, and 1 tbsp of water. Place a lid on the pot and let the chicken cook for 22 mins.
4. Flip the chicken a few times so it cooks evenly then dice the meat into cubes. Now get the following boiling in a separate pot: curry powder, coconut milk, and sugar. Once the mix is boiling set the heat to low, add in the mango, and let the mix gently simmer for 7 mins.
5. Place you rice in a serving dish, and layer the following over each serving: chicken, sprouts, green onions, cashews, and cilantro.
6. Top everything with your curry sauce. Enjoy.

CLASSICAL
Peanut Sauce

Prep Time: 15 mins
Total Time: 15 mins

Servings per Recipe: 16
Calories	160 kcal
Fat	13.7 g
Carbohydrates	5.7g
Protein	6.5 g
Cholesterol	0 mg
Sodium	373 mg

Ingredients

- 1 1/2 C. creamy peanut butter
- 1/2 C. coconut milk
- 3 tbsps water
- 3 tbsps fresh lime juice
- 3 tbsps soy sauce
- 1 tbsp fish sauce
- 1 tbsp hot sauce
- 1 tbsp minced fresh ginger root
- 3 cloves garlic, minced
- 1/4 C. chopped fresh cilantro

Directions

1. Get a bowl, combine: garlic, peanut butter, ginger, coconut milk, hot sauce, water, fish sauce, lime juice, and soy sauce.
2. Stir the mix until it is smooth then add in the cilantro and stir everything again.
3. Enjoy.

Spicy Thai Cabbage and Shrimp

Prep Time: 25 mins
Total Time: 35 mins

Servings per Recipe: 1
Calories	406 kcal
Fat	35.6 g
Carbohydrates	12.1g
Protein	12.3 g
Cholesterol	85 mg
Sodium	1017 mg

Ingredients

- 2 1/2 tbsps vegetable oil
- 1/4 C. water
- 1 C. shredded cabbage
- 1 tbsp minced garlic
- 8 large fresh shrimp, peeled and deveined
- 2 tsps crushed red pepper flakes
- 2 tbsps sliced onion
- 1 tbsp chopped fresh cilantro
- 1 tbsp soy sauce

Directions

1. Begin to stir fry your cabbage with 1 tbsp of water in 1 tbsp of oil for 1 mins.
2. Now place the cabbage to the side.
3. Add in 1.5 tbsp of oil to the pan and begin to stir fry your shrimp and garlic until the fish is fully cooked.
4. Now combine in the rest of the water, pepper, soy sauce, onion, and cilantro.
5. Let the mix fry for half a min then add in the cabbage and get everything hot again.
6. Enjoy.

PAD
Thai III

Prep Time: 30 mins
Total Time: 30 mins

Servings per Recipe: 4
Calories   452 kcal
Fat   28.6 g
Carbohydrates   45.8g
Protein   13.7 g
Cholesterol   0 mg
Sodium   478 mg

Ingredients

2 zucchini, ends trimmed
2 carrots
1 head red cabbage, thinly sliced
1 red bell pepper, thinly sliced
1/2 C. bean sprouts
3/4 C. raw almond butter
2 oranges, juiced
2 tbsps raw honey
1 tbsp minced fresh ginger root
1 tbsp Nama Shoyu (raw soy sauce)
1 tbsp unpasteurized miso
1 clove garlic, minced
1/4 tsp cayenne pepper

Directions

1. Grab a veggie peeler and cut your zucchini lengthwise.
2. Continue cutting the veggies into long streaks to create ribbons.
3. Create the same type of ribbons with your carrots.
4. Now get a bowl, combine: bean sprouts, carrots, bell peppers, and cabbage.
5. Stir the mix to evenly combine everything.
6. Get a 2nd bowl, combine: cayenne, almond butter, orange juice, garlic, miso, honey, Nama Shoyu, and ginger.
7. Add half of the 2nd bowl to the first bowl and stir the mix to evenly coat the veggies.
8. Add your zucchini to the bowl with the cabbage then top the zucchini with the rest of the sauce.
9. Stir everything to evenly distribute the zucchini throughout.
10. Enjoy.

Thai Steak BBQ

Prep Time: 15 mins
Total Time: 3 hrs 25 mins

Servings per Recipe:	8
Calories	160 kcal
Fat	10.7 g
Carbohydrates	1.1g
Protein	< 14 g
Cholesterol	36 mg
Sodium	582 mg

Ingredients

- 1/4 C. chili sauce
- 1/4 C. fish sauce
- 1 1/2 tbsps dark sesame oil
- 1 tbsp grated fresh ginger root
- 3 cloves garlic, peeled and crushed
- 2 lbs flank steak

Directions

1. Get a bowl, combine: garlic, chili sauce, ginger, fish sauce, and sesame oil. Reserve 2 tbsps of the mix then poke some holes in your steak with a large fork then place the meat in the sauce.
2. Flip the steaks to evenly coat them with the marinade then place a covering of plastic over everything.
3. Put the mix in the fridge for 4 hrs.
4. Now get your grill hot and coat the grate with oil.
5. Cook the steaks for 6 mins each side while basting them with the 2 tbsp of reserved sauce.
6. Enjoy.

THAI
Tofu Stir Fry

🥣 Prep Time: 10 mins
🕐 Total Time: 30 mins

Servings per Recipe: 4
Calories   285 kcal
Fat   20.5 g
Carbohydrates   10.6 g
Protein   20.1 g
Cholesterol   0 mg
Sodium   179 mg

Ingredients

- 1 (14 oz.) package firm tofu, cut into 3/4 inch cubes
- 1/3 C. chopped green onion
- 1 1/2 tsps olive oil
- 1/2 tsp sesame oil
- 1 tsp soy sauce
- 2 tsps grated fresh ginger root
- 1/4 C. chunky peanut butter
- 3 tbsps flaked coconut
- sesame seeds

Directions

1. Begin to stir fry your green onions in sesame and olive oil for 60 secs then combine in the tofu and continue frying everything for 5 more mins.
2. After 3 mins of frying top the tofu with your soy sauce and keep frying everything.
3. Now add in your ginger and peanut butter.
4. Stir everything but try to avoid breaking up the tofu by stirring to violently.
5. Shut the heat and add in your coconut.
6. Use the sesame seeds as a garnish.
7. Enjoy.

Sweet Coconut Rice

Prep Time: 5 mins
Total Time: 1 hr

Servings per Recipe: 8
Calories   107 kcal
Fat   0.2 g
Carbohydrates   < 24.4g
Protein   1.4 g
Cholesterol   0 mg
Sodium   7 mg

Ingredients

1/3 C. uncooked glutinous black rice, rinsed
1/2 C. uncooked glutinous white rice, rinsed
1/3 C. palm sugar
3 C. water
1/3 C. coconut cream
1 tsp vanilla extract

Directions

1. Get your two types of rice boiling in water and sugar.
2. Once the mix is boiling, place a lid on the pot, set the heat to low, and cook everything for 50 mins.
3. Stir the mix a few times as it cooks.
4. Now add in your vanilla and coconut cream and stir everything in.
5. Enjoy.

SOUTHEAST Asian Chicken Curry

Prep Time: 20 mins
Total Time: 55 mins

Servings per Recipe: 4
Calories   690 kcal
Fat   41.2 g
Carbohydrates   47.3g
Protein   38.1 g
Cholesterol   73 mg
Sodium   1221 mg

Ingredients

2 tbsps vegetable oil
3 tbsps curry paste
1 (3/4 inch thick) slice ginger, minced
1 1/4 lbs skinless, boneless chicken breast meat - cubed
3 tbsps brown sugar
3 tbsps fish sauce
3 tbsps tamarind paste
1/3 C. peanut butter
3 C. peeled, cubed potatoes
1 (13.5 oz.) can coconut milk
3 tbsps fresh lime juice

Directions

1. Begin to stir fry your ginger and curry paste in veggie oil for 3 mins then add in the chicken and fry everything for 5 mins.
2. Now combine in: the coconut milk, brown sugar, potatoes, fish sauce, peanut butter, and tamarind.
3. Get everything boiling, place a lid on the pot, set the heat to low, and let the mix cook for 22 mins, until the chicken is fully done and the potatoes are soft.
4. Now stir in your lime juice and let the contents cook for 6 more mins.
5. Enjoy.

Tilapia from Thailand

Prep Time: 15 mins
Total Time: 35 mins

Servings per Recipe: 4
Calories   184 kcal
Fat   8.6 g
Carbohydrates   2.4g
Protein   < 24.1 g
Cholesterol   41 mg
Sodium   296 mg

Ingredients

- 1/2 C. coconut milk
- 6 whole almonds
- 2 tbsps chopped white onion
- 1 tsp ground ginger
- 1/2 tsp ground turmeric
- 1 tsp chopped fresh lemon grass
- 1/4 tsp salt
- 4 (4 oz.) fillets tilapia
- salt and pepper to taste
- 1/2 tsp red pepper flakes, or to taste

Directions

1. Puree the following with a food processor: 1/4 tsp salt, coconut milk, lemon grass, almonds, turmeric, onion, and ginger.
2. Begin to fry your fish after coating them with pepper and salt.
3. Top the pieces of fish with the ginger sauce and flip the pieces to make sure everything is coated nicely.
4. Add some pepper flakes over everything and place a lid on the pan.
5. Let the fish cook for 17 mins, with a gentle boil and a low to medium heat.
6. Enjoy.

MAGGIE'S
Easy Thai Style Fried Rice

Prep Time: 15 mins
Total Time: 55 mins

Servings per Recipe: 4
Calories	304 kcal
Fat	12.2 g
Carbohydrates	37.4g
Protein	11.6 g
Cholesterol	68 mg
Sodium	1294 mg

Ingredients

- 2/3 C. uncooked long grain white rice
- 1 1/3 C. water
- 3 tbsps vegetable oil
- 2 medium onions, cut into wedges
- 3 cloves garlic, chopped
- 1/2 tbsp white sugar
- 2 tsps salt
- 1 egg, beaten
- 1/4 lb cooked crabmeat
- 3 green onions, chopped
- 1 tbsp chopped cilantro
- 1/2 cucumber, sliced
- 1 lime, sliced

Directions

1. Get your rice boiling in water, place a lid on the pot, set the heat to low, and let everything cook for 22 mins.
2. Now begin to stir fry your garlic and onions for 7 mins.
3. Once the rice is done add it with the onion mix then also add in the salt and sugar.
4. Let everything continue to cook for 7 more mins while stirring.
5. Combine the eggs with the mix and continue stirring everything until the egg is set into the rice.
6. Now combine in: cilantro, crabmeat, and green onions.
7. Let the mix continue to cook for 6 more mins then top the dish with the pieces of lime and cucumber.
8. Enjoy.

Thai Ginger Fish Patties

Prep Time: 15 mins
Total Time: 55 mins

Servings per Recipe: 6
Calories   319 kcal
Fat   5.6 g
Carbohydrates   32.1g
Protein   33.3 g
Cholesterol   82 mg
Sodium   596 mg

Ingredients

- 1 1/2 lbs fresh tuna steaks, minced
- 1/2 C. dry bread crumbs
- 1/4 C. finely chopped green onion
- 1/4 C. grated carrot
- 1 tbsp minced fresh ginger root
- 1 tbsp chopped fresh cilantro
- 1 tsp sesame oil
- 1 tbsp ketchup
- 1 tbsp lite soy sauce
- 1/2 tsp ground cumin
- 1/4 tsp salt
- 1/4 tsp black pepper
- 1 egg, beaten
- 6 hamburger buns
- 6 lettuce leaves - rinsed and dried
- 2 medium tomatoes, sliced

Directions

1. Get a bowl, combine: egg, tuna, pepper, bread crumbs, salt, green onions, cumin, carrots, soy sauce, ginger, ketchup, sesame oil, and cilantro.
2. Place a covering of plastic on the bowl and put everything in the fridge for 40 mins.
3. Now get the broiler of your oven hot before doing anything else.
4. Shape the mix into 6 burgers then put everything in a broiler pan.
5. Broil the patties for 5 mins each side.
6. Place your patties on some buns then top them with some tomato and lettuce.
7. Enjoy.

FISH CAKES
from Thailand

Prep Time: 10 mins
Total Time: 30 mins

Servings per Recipe: 8
Calories	164 kcal
Fat	6.9 g
Carbohydrates	11.9 g
Protein	13 g
Cholesterol	57 mg
Sodium	155 mg

Ingredients

1 lb boneless fish fillets, cubed
1/2 C. all-purpose flour
2 tbsps oyster sauce
2 tbsps sweet chili sauce
1 tsp fish sauce
1 tsp brown sugar
1/4 C. chopped fresh cilantro
4 green onions, sliced

1 egg
all-purpose flour
oil for frying

Directions

1. Puree the following in a food processor: egg, fish, green onions, half C. flour, oyster sauce, cilantro, sweet chili sauce, brown sugar, and fish sauce.
2. Form the mix into burgers then coat each one with some flour.
3. Get half an inch of oil hot and ready for frying before doing anything else.
4. Now begin to cook the burgers for 4 mins then flip them and cook the patties for 5 more mins.
5. Enjoy.

Nam Prik Ong (Lettuce Topped with Curry Turkey)

Prep Time: 5 mins
Total Time: 30 mins

Servings per Recipe: 6
Calories   452 kcal
Fat   32.2 g
Carbohydrates   12.6g
Protein   27.1 g
Cholesterol   109 mg
Sodium   592 mg

Ingredients

- 1/4 C. white rice
- 2 lbs ground turkey
- 1 red onion, finely chopped
- 2 tbsps red curry paste (such as Mae Ploy)
- 2 tbsps tomato paste
- 1/4 C. water (optional)
- 2 limes, juiced
- 2 tbsps fish sauce
- 12 leaves lettuce

Directions

1. Get your rice frying in a pan until it's toasted and brown all over.
2. Do this without oil for a few mins. Now place the rice in a food processor and puree it into a powder. Begin to fry your turkey for 6 mins or until done then add in the onions and keep frying everything until the onions are see-through. Add in the curry paste and heat it until becomes fragrant then add the tomatoes and get everything gently boiling.
3. Once the mix is gently boiling add in 1/4 C. of water if the mix is a bit too dry, if not you can skip this step.
4. Now combine in the powdered rice and the cook the mix for 6 mins before adding the fish sauce and lime juice in line with your preferences.
5. Place your pieces of lettuce on a serving plate then top the leaves with the turkey mix.
6. Enjoy.

HONEY and Chili Chicken Legs

Prep Time: 10 mins
Total Time: 1 hr 30 mins

Servings per Recipe: 12
Calories   142 kcal
Fat   4.1 g
Carbohydrates   5.9 g
Protein   19.6 g
Cholesterol   62 mg
Sodium   353 mg

Ingredients

2 tbsps honey
5 tbsps sweet chili sauce
3 tbsps soy sauce

12 chicken drumsticks, skin removed

Directions

1. Get a bowl, combine: soy sauce, honey, and sweet chili sauce. Reserve some of the mix for later.
2. Add your pieces of chicken to the mix, place a covering of plastic around the bowl and put everything in the fridge for 65 mins.
3. Now get your grill hot and coat the grate with some oil.
4. Cook the chicken on the grill for 11 mins each side while coating the meat with the reserved marinade.
5. Enjoy.

Bangkok Ginger Beef

Prep Time: 15 mins
Total Time: 1 hr 40 mins

Servings per Recipe: 6
Calories   183 kcal
Fat   4.9 g
Carbohydrates   20.4g
Protein   14.6 g
Cholesterol   25 mg
Sodium   634 mg

Ingredients

- 2 tbsps coriander seeds, coarsely cracked
- 1/2 C. firmly packed dark brown sugar
- 1/4 C. soy sauce
- 1 tbsp lime juice
- 2 cloves garlic, minced
- 1 pinch ground ginger
- 1 1/2 lbs flank steak, frozen for 40 mins

Directions

1. Get a bowl, combine: ground ginger, coriander, garlic, brown sugar, lime juice, and soy sauce.
2. Stir the mix until it is smooth then cut your steak along the grain and add the steak into the mix.
3. Place a covering of plastic on the bowl and put everything in the fridge for 60 mins.
4. Now get your oven's broiler hot.
5. Place your pieces of meat in a broiler pan coated with foil and broil the meat for 5 mins while coating the meat with the reserved sauce.
6. Enjoy.

THAI Pizza

Prep Time: 15 mins
Total Time: 27 mins

Servings per Recipe: 12
Calories	554 kcal
Fat	28.3 g
Carbohydrates	43.2g
Protein	34.9 g
Cholesterol	54 mg
Sodium	741 mg

Ingredients

1 tbsp vegetable oil
2 skinless, boneless chicken breast halves, chopped
1 C. prepared Thai peanut sauce
1 bunch green onions, chopped

4 small (4 inch) pita breads
4 slices provolone cheese

Directions

1. Stir fry your pieces of chicken in oil for 9 mins.
2. Now set your oven to 425 degrees before doing anything else.
3. Evenly divide the following amongst your pieces of pita: peanut sauce, scallions and chicken.
4. Place one piece of cheese on each one and put everything on a baking sheet.
5. Cook everything in the oven for 13 mins.
6. Enjoy.

Filipino Oxtail Stew

Prep Time: 2 hrs 20 mins
Total Time: 2 hrs 35 mins

Servings per Recipe: 6
Calories   395 kcal
Carbohydrates   14.9 g
Cholesterol   125 mg
Fat   21 g
Protein   40.1 g
Sodium   683 mg

Ingredients

- 1 1/2 pounds beef oxtail, cut into pieces
- 1 large onion, quartered
- 2 cloves garlic, chopped
- 1 tsp salt
- 1/2 tsp ground black pepper, or to taste
- 1 large eggplant, cut into 2-inch chunks
- 1/2 head bok choy, cut into 1-inch pieces
- 1/2 pound fresh green beans, trimmed and snapped into 2-inch pieces
- 1/4 C. peanut butter, or as needed to thicken sauce

Directions

1. Bring the mixture of oxtail pieces, pepper, garlic and salt to boil in water before cooking it for two hours over medium heat.
2. Now add eggplant, green beans and bok choy into this mixture before cooking it for another 20 minutes or until the vegetables you just added are tender.
3. Add a mixture of peanut butter and some broth into the stew just before you serve it.

BUKO I
(Coconut Chiller)

Prep Time: 15 mins
Total Time: 15 mins

Servings per Recipe: 2
Calories	1430 kcal
Carbohydrates	66.7 g
Cholesterol	0 mg
Fat	133 g
Protein	13.2 g
Sodium	87 mg

Ingredients

2 fresh young coconuts
1 C. water
1 tbsp white sugar, or to taste
ice cubes

Directions

1. Cut the top of a coconut and pour its juice into a bowl.
2. Slice the coconut into two pieces and scrap out its inner flesh into the bowl containing the juice.
3. Now mix sugar and some water, and pour it over ice in a glass.
4. Serve.

Biko
(Filipino Sweet Baked Rice)

Prep Time: 15 mins
Total Time: 11 hrs

Servings per Recipe: 6
Calories   463 kcal
Carbohydrates   90.3 g
Cholesterol   0 mg
Fat   9.5 g
Protein   5.4 g
Sodium   17 mg

Ingredients

- 4 C. uncooked glutinous white rice
- 6 C. cold water
- 1 (14 ounce) can coconut milk, divided
- 1 1/3 C. white sugar
- 1 1/3 C. brown sugar
- 3 tbsps coconut preserves (such as Phil Supreme)

Directions

1. Preheat your oven to 325 degrees F and grease the baking pan.
2. Cook rice that has been soaked in water for at least 8 hours along with half a C. of coconut milk, white sugar and water until the rice is tender.
3. Now pour this mixture into the already prepared baking pan and pour a boiled mixture of coconut milk, brown sugar and coconut preserves over the rice.
4. Bake in the preheated oven for about 25 minutes and cut into squares.
5. Serve.

TULYA

Prep Time: 15 mins
Total Time: 25 mins

Servings per Recipe: 6
Calories   120 kcal
Carbohydrates   5.3 g
Cholesterol   20 mg
Fat   7.4 g
Protein   8.1 g
Sodium   91 mg

Ingredients

2 tbsps olive oil
1 onion, chopped
2 cloves garlic, minced
1 (2 inch) piece fresh ginger, peeled and grated
2 tbsps oyster sauce
1/2 C. water
2 1/4 pounds clams in shell, scrubbed

Directions

1. Cook onion, garlic and ginger in hot oil for about 5 minutes before adding oyster sauce and cooking for another 2 minutes.
2. Pour water into the mix and cook for another two minutes while covering the pan.
3. Now add clams and cook for another 5 minutes or until the clams have opened up.
4. Discard all the unopened clams and serve.

Chicken Adobo

Prep Time: 1 hr
Total Time: 1 hr 15 mins

Servings per Recipe: 6
Calories   340 kcal
Carbohydrates   2 g
Cholesterol   100 mg
Fat   21.5 g
Protein   32.5 g
Sodium   3598 mg

Ingredients

- 1 1/2 C. water
- 1 C. distilled white vinegar
- 4 tbsps soy sauce
- 1 tsp whole peppercorns
- 4 cloves garlic, crushed
- 2 tbsps salt
- 1 (2 to 3 pound) whole chicken, cut into pieces
- 2 tbsps vegetable oil

Directions

1. Mix water, salt, vinegar, peppercorns, garlic and soy sauce before adding chicken and cooking it over low heat for about 30 minutes or until the chicken is tender.
2. Cook this chicken in hot oil until brown after removing it from the pot.
3. Now put this chicken back into the pot and cook over medium heat until you see that the liquid has become thick.
4. Serve.

BARBECUED
Spareribs

Prep Time: 10 mins
Total Time: 1 hr 10 mins

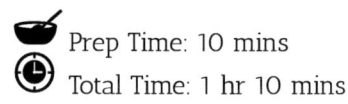

Servings per Recipe: 2
Calories	710 kcal
Carbohydrates	20.6 g
Cholesterol	192 mg
Fat	48.4 g
Protein	46.1 g
Sodium	765 mg

Ingredients

1 (4 pound) package beef spareribs, rinsed and patted dry
salt and ground black pepper to taste
1 C. water
1 C. sweet chili sauce

Directions

1. Preheat your oven to 350 degrees F and grease the baking pan.
2. Add some salt and pepper over spareribs before putting them into the baking dish containing water.
3. Cover with aluminum foil.
4. Bake in the preheated oven for about 30 minutes before pouring chili sauce half of what we have and return it to the oven.
5. Brush with chili sauce every five minutes and continue baking for 30 more minutes or until tender.
6. Serve.

Empanada Turkey Filling

Prep Time: 10 mins
Total Time: 1 hr 25 mins

Servings per Recipe: 6
Calories   67 kcal
Carbohydrates   4.4 g
Cholesterol   12 mg
Fat   3.9 g
Protein   4 g
Sodium   19 mg

Ingredients

1 pound ground turkey
salt and pepper to taste
2 tbsps olive oil
1 onion, chopped
2 cloves garlic, minced
1 (9 ounce) box frozen peas and carrots
1 (1.5 ounce) box raisins
1 small potato, diced

Directions

1. Take out ground turkey and cook it over medium heat in nonstick skillet for about 5 minutes or until you see that it is brown.
2. Now cook onion and garlic in hot oil for about 5 minutes before adding browned turkey into it and cooking it for another 5 minutes.
3. Now add potato, raisins, peas and carrots into the skillet, and cook them for about 10 minutes or until the vegetables are tender.
4. Allow this to cool down before filling into empanada dough.
5. Serve.

FILIPINO
Melon Dessert I

🥣 Prep Time: 20 mins
🕐 Total Time: 1 day

Servings per Recipe: 6
Calories   123 kcal
Carbohydrates   30.5 g
Cholesterol   0 mg
Fat   0.6 g
Protein   2.3 g
Sodium   70 mg

Ingredients

1 large ripe cantaloupe
2 quarts cold water
1 large honeydew melon

Directions

1. Blend cantaloupe and place it in a pitcher.
2. Now pour into it some water and refrigerate it for 12 hours or preferably overnight.
3. Make small balls out of the honeydew melon using a spoon and add these balls before serving.

Salmon Stew (Abalos Style)

Prep Time: 10 mins
Total Time: 25 mins

Servings per Recipe: 4
Calories   223 kcal
Carbohydrates   4.8 g
Cholesterol   45 mg
Fat   11 g
Protein   24.9 g
Sodium   466 mg

Ingredients

- 1 tbsp olive oil
- 4 cloves garlic, minced
- 1 onion, diced
- 1 tomato, diced
- 1 (14.75 ounce) can pink salmon
- 2 1/2 C. water
- bay leaf (optional)
- salt and ground black pepper to taste
- 1 tsp fish sauce (optional)

Directions

1. Cook onion and garlic in hot oil for about 5 minutes before adding tomato and salmon into it.
2. Cook for another 3 minutes and then add water, fish sauce, bay leaf, salt and pepper.
3. Cover the skillet and cook for 20 minutes.
4. Serve.

FRIED
Tulingan (Mackerel)

Prep Time: 10 mins
Total Time: 1 hr 50 mins

Servings per Recipe: 4
Calories 974 kcal
Carbohydrates 0.8 g
Cholesterol 222 mg
Fat 70 g
Protein 77.6 g
Sodium 841 mg

Ingredients

1 (3 1/2) pound whole mackerel, gutted and cleaned
2 C. water
1 tbsp tamarind soup base
1 tsp fish sauce
oil for frying

Directions

1. Mix mackerel water, fish sauce and a tamarind soup base in a skillet, and cook over medium heat for about 15 minutes.
2. Flip the fish once very carefully and cook for another 15 minutes before turning off the heat and letting it stand as it is for about one hour.
3. Take out the fish and dry it with paper towels before deep frying it in large skillet for about 10 minutes.
4. Serve.

Filipino Fruit Salad

Prep Time: 10 mins
Total Time: 1 hr 10 mins

Servings per Recipe: 10
Calories   482 kcal
Carbohydrates   61.8 g
Cholesterol   23 mg
Fat   25.9 g
Protein   9.8 g
Sodium   204 mg

Ingredients

- 1 (30 ounce) can fruit cocktail, drained
- 1 (15 ounce) can lychees, drained
- 1 (12 ounce) jar macapuno (coconut preserves), drained
- 1 (20 ounce) can palm seeds, drained
- 1 (15 ounce) can creamed corn
- 1 Red Delicious apple, cored and diced
- 1 Asian pear, cored and cubed
- 1 (8 ounce) container sour cream
- 1 (14 ounce) can sweetened condensed milk

Directions

1. Combine all the ingredients mentioned above in a bowl and serve it cold.

AVOCADO
Milkshakes in the Philippines

🥣 Prep Time: 5 mins
🕐 Total Time: 5 mins

Servings per Recipe: 6
Calories			336 kcal
Carbohydrates	37.6 g
Cholesterol		18 mg
Fat				19.1 g
Protein			7.8 g
Sodium			84 mg

Ingredients

1 avocado - peeled, pitted, and cubed
5 cubes ice
3 tbsps white sugar
1 1/3 C. milk
1 tsp fresh lemon or lime juice
1 scoop vanilla ice cream

Directions

1. Blend all the ingredients mentioned above in a blender until required smoothness is achieved.
2. Serve.

Singkamas (Jicama Salad)

Prep Time: 30 mins
Total Time: 1 hr 30 mins

Servings per Recipe: 10
Calories	113 kcal
Carbohydrates	27.5 g
Cholesterol	0 mg
Fat	0.2 g
Protein	1.4 g
Sodium	244 mg

Ingredients

- 1 large jicama, peeled and cut into matchsticks
- 1 red bell pepper, cut into long thin strips
- 1 green bell pepper, cut into long thin strips
- 1 small red onion, sliced into thin lengthwise slivers
- 2 green chile peppers, halved lengthwise, seeded, and cut into strips
- 1 (2 inch) piece fresh ginger root, thinly sliced
- 1 carrot, cut into matchsticks
- 1 C. water
- 2/3 C. vinegar
- 2/3 C. white sugar
- 1 tsp salt

Directions

1. Mix jicama, red bell pepper, red onion, green chili peppers, ginger, green bell pepper and carrot in large sized bowl.
2. In another bowl, mix water, salt, vinegar and sugar.
3. Pour this mixture over the vegetables and refrigerate it for about 1 hour at least before serving it.

PICADILLO
Filipino (Hamburger Abalos Soup)

Prep Time: 20 mins
Total Time: 1 hr 5 mins

Servings per Recipe: 6
Calories   233 kcal
Carbohydrates   16.9 g
Cholesterol   46 mg
Fat   11.5 g
Protein   15.4 g
Sodium   862 mg

Ingredients

1 tbsp cooking oil
1 onion, diced
4 cloves garlic, minced
1 large tomato, diced
1 pound ground beef
4 C. water
1 large potato, diced
2 tbsps beef bouillon
2 tbsps fish sauce
salt and pepper to taste

Directions

1. Cook onions and garlic in hot oil over medium heat until tender add tomatoes and cook for another 3 minutes.
2. Now add ground beef and cook for about 5 more minutes or until the color has turned brown.
3. Add potato, fish sauce, pepper, beef bouillon, water and some salt into the pan and cook at low heat for 30 minutes while stirring regularly.
4. Serve.

Fish Sinigang (Tilapia)

- Prep Time: 5 mins
- Total Time: 15 mins

Servings per Recipe: 10
Calories	112 kcal
Carbohydrates	13.4 g
Cholesterol	21 mg
Fat	1 g
Protein	13.1 g
Sodium	63 mg

Ingredients

- 1/2 pound tilapia fillets, cut into chunks
- 1 small head bok choy, chopped
- 2 medium tomatoes, cut into chunks
- 1 C. thinly sliced daikon radish
- 1/4 C. tamarind paste
- 3 C. water
- 2 dried red chile peppers (optional)

Directions

1. Combine tilapia, radish, tomatoes, mixture of tamarind paste and water, chili peppers and bok choy.
2. Bring the mixture to boil and cook for 5 minutes to get fish tender.
3. Serve in appropriate bowls.

SINIGANG NA BAKA
(Beef Based Veggie Soup)

Prep Time: 15 mins
Total Time: 1 hr

Servings per Recipe: 6
Calories 304 kcal
Carbohydrates 15 g
Cholesterol 51 mg
Fat 19.7 g
Protein 17.8 g
Sodium 1405 mg

Ingredients

2 tbsps canola oil
1 large onion, chopped
2 cloves garlic, chopped
1 pound beef stew meat, cut into 1 inch cubes
1 quart water
2 large tomatoes, diced
1/2 pound fresh green beans, rinsed and trimmed
1/2 medium head bok choy, cut into 1 1/2 inch strips
1 head fresh broccoli, cut into bite size pieces
1 (1.41 ounce) package tamarind soup base

Directions

1. Cook onion and garlic in hot oil and then add beef to get it brown.
2. Now add some water and bring it to a boil.
3. Turn the heat down to medium and cook for 30 minutes.
4. Cook for another 10 minutes after adding tomatoes and green beans.
5. Now add tamarind soup mix, bok choy and some broccoli into the mix and cook for 10 more minutes to get everything tender.

Melon Chiller

Prep Time: 20 mins
Total Time: 1 hr 5 mins

Servings per Recipe: 6
Calories   174 kcal
Carbohydrates   44.5 g
Cholesterol   0 mg
Fat   0.1 g
Protein   0.5 g
Sodium   23 mg

Ingredients

- 1 cantaloupe, halved and seeded
- 1 gallon water
- 2 C. white sugar
- ice cubes, as needed

Directions

1. Take out the meat of cantaloupe and place into a punch bowl with a melon baller add sugar and some water after placing this into bowl.
2. Mix it well and serve it cold.

FILIPINO
Chicken Stew

Prep Time: 25 mins
Total Time: 1 hr 5 mins

Servings per Recipe: 8
Calories	554 kcal
Carbohydrates	28.4 g
Cholesterol	57 mg
Fat	32.3 g
Protein	28.4 g
Sodium	645 mg

Ingredients

2 tbsps sesame oil
2 pounds boneless chicken pieces, cut into strips
2 tbsps fresh lemon juice
2 tbsps soy sauce
2 (15 ounce) cans coconut milk
1/4 C. red curry paste
1/4 C. flour
2 red bell peppers, chopped
1 sweet onion, chopped
1 red onion, chopped
2 cloves garlic, minced
2 large potatoes, cubed
2 (8 ounce) cans sliced bamboo shoots, drained
2 (8 ounce) cans sliced water chestnuts, drained
2 (8 ounce) cans baby corn, drained
1 (12 ounce) can sliced mushrooms, drained
1/4 C. chopped cilantro

Directions

1. Cook chicken, lemon juice, and soy sauce in hot sesame oil over medium heat for 5 minutes and in a bowl mix flour, coconut milk and curry paste, and add this mixture to the pan.
2. Now put bell pepper, red onion, garlic, potatoes, bamboo shoots, water chestnuts, sweet onion and mushrooms into the pan and cook at low heat for 45 minutes before adding cilantro and removing it from heat.
3. Serve

Champorado

Prep Time: 5 mins
Total Time: 35 mins

Servings per Recipe: 6
Calories   428 kcal
Carbohydrates   53.4 g
Cholesterol   0 mg
Fat   25.2 g
Protein   4.9 g
Sodium   407 mg

Ingredients

- 1 C. glutinous sweet rice
- 2 C. light coconut milk
- 1/2 C. cocoa powder
- 1 C. white sugar
- 1 tsp salt
- 1 C. thick coconut milk

Directions

1. Bring the mixture of sweet rice and coconut milk to boil for 10 minutes while stirring regularly.
2. Now add sugar, salt and cocoa power into this rice and cook at low heat for about 10 minutes or until you see that the rice is tender.
3. Pour thick coconut milk into it and serve.

MAJA Blanca Maiz (Corn Pudding)

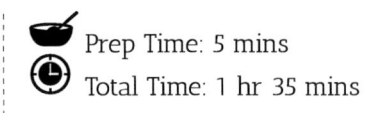

Prep Time: 5 mins
Total Time: 1 hr 35 mins

Servings per Recipe: 8
Calories   239 kcal
Carbohydrates   41.1 g
Cholesterol   0 mg
Fat   8.4 g
Protein   2.4 g
Sodium   121 mg

Ingredients

- 1 2/3 C. coconut milk
- 1 (14.5 ounce) can cream-style corn
- 1 C. rice flour
- 1 C. white sugar

Directions

1. Mix all the ingredients mentioned above thoroughly in a pan over medium heat and cook for 30 minutes or until the required thickness is achieved.
2. Now pour everything into a serving platter and let it cool.
3. Serve.

Cassava Cake

Prep Time: 20 mins
Total Time: 2 hrs 20 mins

Servings per Recipe: 1
Calories   329 kcal
Carbohydrates   41.6 g
Cholesterol   60 mg
Fat   15.5 g
Protein   8 g
Sodium   111 mg

Ingredients

- 2 C. grated, peeled yucca
- 2 eggs, beaten
- 1 (12 ounce) can evaporated milk
- 1 (14 ounce) can sweetened condensed milk
- 1 (14 ounce) can coconut milk

Directions

1. Set your oven to 350 degrees F before continuing.
2. Mix all the ingredients mentioned above in a bowl and pour this mixture into a baking dish.
3. Bake this for one hour before switching on the broiler and letting it turn the top of the cake brown.
4. Refrigerate before serving.

BUTTER Cookies in the Philippines

Prep Time: 5 mins
Total Time: 17 mins

Servings per Recipe: 60
Calories   74 kcal
Carbohydrates   10.5 g
Cholesterol   17 mg
Fat   3.3 g
Protein   0.4 g
Sodium   34 mg

Ingredients

1 C. butter, softened
1 C. white sugar
3 eggs
3 2/3 C. cornstarch
1 tsp cream of tartar
1 tsp baking powder

Directions

1. Set your oven at 350 degrees F and grease the cookie sheets before continuing.
2. Mix butter and sugar, and then add eggs one by one.
3. Now add cornstarch, cream of tartar and some baking powder.
4. Mix them well and place 1 inch balls over the greased cookie sheets.
5. Bake this for 12 minutes in the preheated oven and then let it cool down before serving.

Filipino Melon Dessert II

Prep Time: 15 mins
Total Time: 6 hrs 15 mins

Servings per Recipe: 20
Calories	105 kcal
Carbohydrates	21.8 g
Cholesterol	5 mg
Fat	1.6 g
Protein	2 g
Sodium	37 mg

Ingredients

- 4 pounds cantaloupe, shredded
- 1 (12 fluid ounce) can of evaporated milk
- 2 quarts water
- 1 1/4 C. white sugar

Directions

1. Mix all the ingredients mentioned above thoroughly and then refrigerate for some time.
2. Divide this into molds and freeze this for about 6 hours or until it is firm enough.

CHOCOLATE-ORANGE
Rice Pudding

Prep Time: 10 mins
Total Time: 50 mins

Servings per Recipe: 8
Calories	356 kcal
Carbohydrates	60.6 g
Cholesterol	13 mg
Fat	9.7 g
Protein	8.3 g
Sodium	72 mg

Ingredients

5 1/2 C. milk
1 C. Arborio rice
2/3 C. white sugar
2 tbsps orange juice
1 1/2 tsps grated orange zest

2 tbsps orange liqueur
1 tbsp unsweetened cocoa powder
1 C. semisweet chocolate chips

Directions

1. Mix rice, orange zest, milk and orange juice in a pan and bring it to a boil before turning down the heat to medium and cooking for another 40 minutes or until the rice is tender.
2. Add orange liqueur and cocoa powder into the rice mixture after removing it from the heat.
3. Also add some chocolate chips and let it melt.
4. Serve.

Corned Beef Hash In the Philippines

Prep Time: 15 mins
Total Time: 45 mins

Servings per Recipe: 4
Calories	333 kcal
Carbohydrates	21.1 g
Cholesterol	72 mg
Fat	16.2 g
Protein	25.5 g
Sodium	853 mg

Ingredients

- 1 tbsp vegetable oil
- 4 cloves garlic, chopped
- 1 onion, diced
- 1 tomato, chopped
- 1 large potato, diced
- 1 (12 ounce) can corned beef
- salt and pepper to taste

Directions

1. Cook onion and garlic over in hot oil over medium heat and then add tomatoes and potatoes.
2. Cook for 10 minutes and then add beef, and cook for another 10 minutes.
3. Add some salt and pepper before serving.
4. Enjoy.

CORNED BEEF
Waffles

Prep Time: 10 mins
Total Time: 20 mins

Servings per Recipe: 10
Calories	148 kcal
Carbohydrates	16 g
Cholesterol	54 mg
Fat	5.2 g
Protein	8.8 g
Sodium	268 mg

Ingredients

2 eggs
1 1/4 C. milk
2 tsps cooking oil
1 1/2 C. all-purpose flour
1 pinch salt
2 tsps baking powder
1/2 (12 ounce) can corned beef, broken into pieces

Directions

1. Heat a waffle iron before continuing.
2. Combine milk, oil and eggs in a bowl and in a separate bowl mix flour salt and baking powder.
3. Combine both mixtures and add beef.
4. Put this mixture into the preheated waffle iron and cook it until the waffles are golden in color.
5. Serve it with butter.

Mango Bread

Prep Time: 20 mins
Total Time: 1 hr 20 mins

Servings per Recipe: 2
Calories	193 kcal
Carbohydrates	27.2 g
Cholesterol	19 mg
Fat	8.9 g
Protein	2.1 g
Sodium	192 mg

Ingredients

- 2 C. all-purpose flour
- 2 tsps ground cinnamon
- 2 tsps baking soda
- 1/2 tsp salt
- 1 1/4 C. white sugar
- 2 eggs
- 3/4 C. vegetable oil
- 2 1/2 C. mangos, peeled, seeded and chopped
- 1 tsp lemon juice
- 1/4 C. raisins

Directions

1. Mix all the dry ingredients mentioned above and then add eggs beaten in oil to this mixture.
2. Now add mangoes, raisins and lemon.
3. Pour this into two different pans and bake at 350 degrees F for 60 minutes.
4. Serve.

GUINATAAN
Hito (Catfish)

Prep Time: 10 mins
Total Time: 40 mins

Servings per Recipe: 4
Calories	388 kcal
Carbohydrates	5.4 g
Cholesterol	51 mg
Fat	33.2 g
Protein	19.1 g
Sodium	64 mg

Ingredients

2 tbsps cooking oil
1 onion, chopped
2 cloves garlic, crushed
4 (4 ounce) catfish fillets
salt and pepper to taste
1 1/2 C. coconut milk

Directions

1. Cook onion and garlic in hot oil for about 10 minutes and then add catfish, and cook for another 2 minutes.
2. Now add coconut milk and cook for another 10 minutes or until the coconut milk gets oily.
3. Serve with rice.

Buko II
(Filipino Coconut Pie Dessert)

Prep Time: 20 mins
Total Time: 1 hr 5 mins

Servings per Recipe: 6
Calories	693 kcal
Carbohydrates	66.9 g
Cholesterol	183 mg
Fat	40.7 g
Protein	20.1 g
Sodium	276 mg

Ingredients

- 1 fresh young coconut, drained with meat removed and chopped
- 2 (12 fluid ounce) cans of evaporated milk
- 1 (14 ounce) can sweetened condensed milk
- 4 eggs, beaten
- 1/4 C. white sugar
- 1 pinch salt

Directions

1. Set your oven to 350 degrees F before continuing.
2. Now combine all the ingredients mentioned above in a large bowl and pour into a baking dish.
3. Fill the baking with enough water to cover half.
4. Now bake everything in the preheated oven for about 60 minutes.
5. Cool it down and serve.

ENJOY THE RECIPES?

KEEP ON COOKING WITH 6 MORE FREE COOKBOOKS!

Visit our website and simply enter your email address to join the club and receive your 6 cookbooks.

http://booksumo.com/magnet

https://www.instagram.com/booksumopress/

https://www.facebook.com/booksumo/

Printed in Great Britain
by Amazon